STRANGE Life Cycles

The Bizarre Life Cycle of a CICADA

By Greg Roza

Gareth Stevens
Publishing

Please visit our website, www.garethstevens.com. For a free color catalog of all our high-quality books, call toll free 1-800-542-2595 or fax 1-877-542-2596.

Library of Congress Cataloging-in-Publication Data

Roza, Greg.
The bizarre life cycle of a cicada / Greg Roza.
    p. cm. — (Strange life cycles)
Includes index.
ISBN 978-1-4339-7040-5 (pbk.)
ISBN 978-1-4339-7041-2 (6-pack)
ISBN 978-1-4339-7039-9 (library binding)
1. Cicadas—Life cycles—Juvenile literature. I. Title. II. Series: Roza, Greg. Strange life cycles.
QL527.C5R69 2012
595.7'52—dc23

                              2011050605

First Edition

Published in 2013 by
Gareth Stevens Publishing
111 East 14th Street, Suite 349
New York, NY 10003

Designer: Andrea Davison-Bartolotta
Editor: Kristen Rajczak

Photo credits: Cover, pp. 1, 4, 6, 10, 11, 15, 17 Shutterstock.com; pp. 5, 13, 19, 20 iStockphoto.com; p. 7 iStockphoto/Thinkstock; p. 8 Paul Whitten/Photo Researchers/Getty Images; p. 9 Wood/Custom Medical Stock Photo/Getty Images; p. 16 James H. Robinson/Photo Researchers/Getty Images.

Printed in the United States of America

CPSIA compliance information: Batch #CS12GS: For further information contact Gareth Stevens, New York, New York at 1-800-542-2595.

Contents

Words in the glossary appear in **bold** type the first time they are used in the text.

Buzz Buzz

Have you ever heard a loud buzzing on a summer day? It was probably a cicada (suh-KAY-duh). Actually, it was probably a lot of cicadas! They're some of the loudest insects in the world.

Cicadas have large bodies with six legs. They have two small wings and two large, **transparent** wings. They have two bulging eyes with three smaller eyes between them. The most interesting thing about cicadas is their life cycle. It's truly bizarre!

THE FACTS OF LIFE

There are more than 2,000 cicada **species** in the world. More than 100 species live in North America.

Cicadas have bodies that are commonly black or dark brown.

Friend or Foe?

Cicadas are big bugs. Adults can be up to 2.25 inches (5.7 cm) long. A flying cicada can be a creepy sight! But don't worry—cicadas don't bite.

Cicadas are actually good for people. Young cicadas dig tunnels in the earth. This lets air into the ground and makes it good for plants. Dead cicadas break down and put important **nutrients** into the soil. They also provide food for many animals.

THE FACTS OF LIFE

Many people think cicadas are bad for vegetable crops. However, adult cicadas mainly eat tree sap.

An adult cicada holds on to a twig with its six legs.

Young Cicadas

Cicadas begin life as tiny, wingless **larvae** called nymphs. They break out of eggs that female cicadas have laid in the stems of plants and tree branches. The nymphs fall to the ground and **burrow** up to 2 feet (61 cm) into the earth. Depending on the species, the nymphs remain underground for 2 to 17 years.

Nymphs stay alive by eating sap from tree roots. They **shed** their skin several times as they grow. Some are eaten by beetle larvae before they finish growing up.

THE FACTS OF LIFE

Beetle larvae aren't a nymph's only natural enemy. Birds and wasps eat nymphs, too.

This cicada nymph has been underground for 3 years!

Here They Come!

In time, cicada nymphs use their strong front legs to crawl out of the ground. Millions of cicadas—called a brood—crawl out of the ground at the same time. This usually happens at night. In areas where it gets cold in winter, cicadas **emerge** in May when the soil has warmed up.

These young cicadas are pale and have a soft **exoskeleton**. They climb up trees and shed their skin for the last time, becoming adults. The exoskeleton hardens and darkens as they rest.

THE FACTS OF LIFE

In some cicada species, new cicadas appear every year. However, nymphs take years to **mature**, and the newly emerged cicadas have been growing underground for several years.

You may find hundreds of dried exoskeletons shed by cicadas on trees after a brood emerges.

Short Life

Adult cicadas live up to about 6 weeks. They spend much of this time on trees. Cicadas have a long mouthpart they keep tucked against their body. The mouthpart has four tiny tubes. Cicadas use these needlelike tubes to suck sap out of trees.

Adult cicadas have many enemies. These include birds and squirrels. Since so many cicadas emerge in one brood, there's a lot of food to go around. Even after cicadas' enemies have eaten their fill, there are still plenty of cicadas left to lay eggs.

THE FACTS OF LIFE

There are two main kinds of cicadas in North America. New dog-day cicadas emerge every year. Periodical cicadas emerge once every 13 or 17 years.

A cicada is caught by one of its natural enemies—a bird.

Sing Me a Song

Male cicadas are well known for their "singing." Males make a loud buzzing to **attract** females. They do this with special parts on their exoskeleton called tymbals. The sound a male makes is a **mating** call. Females hear the sound and find the males.

All male cicadas in a brood usually produce their mating call at the same time. This can get very loud. The sound hurts birds' ears, which helps keep them away during mating season.

THE FACTS OF LIFE

Each cicada species has its own special mating call.

Cicadas only mate once in their lives.

Mama Cicada

After mating, the female cicada finds a tree. She uses a sharp spike on her belly to make a cut in a twig. She lays 24 to 28 eggs in the cut and moves on to make another cut. This process continues until she has laid all her eggs. Each female cicada lays between 400 and 600 eggs.

The eggs take 4 to 8 weeks to hatch—and the cycle starts all over again!

cicada eggs

Female cicadas sometimes cause harm to young apple and pear trees when they lay their eggs.

Mother cicadas don't live long after laying their eggs.

I Can't Take the Noise!

All broods don't come aboveground at the same time. This is because different species spend different amounts of time underground.

You may not notice cicadas every summer unless you go looking for them. Some years, the broods are small and you may not hear them at all. During summers when a larger number of broods appear, you'll be sure to hear the males singing. They can be so loud you may want to cover your ears and shut your windows!

THE FACTS OF LIFE

At close range, some larger species of cicadas can create sounds around 120 **decibels**. That's about as loud as an ambulance siren!

When a brood emerges, it may cover cars and the walls of buildings, and some may even fly into people's hair!

19

Periodical Cicadas

There are seven species of periodical cicadas in the eastern United States. Periodical cicadas appear once every 13 or 17 years. Scientists use roman numerals to keep track of periodical broods. Some broods occupy a small area when they appear. Others extend across several states. There are 12 broods of 17-year cicadas and three broods of 13-year cicadas.

Some people find the sudden appearance of so many cicadas bizarre and creepy. Others, however, enjoy this rare but loud bug show.

Don't be afraid! Cicadas won't hurt you.

Periodical Cicadas in the United States

17-year broods

brood	one appearance	next appearance
I	2012	2029
II	2013	2030
III	2014	2031
IV	2015	2032
V	2016	2033
VI	2017	2034
VII	2001	2018
VIII	2002	2019
IX	2003	2020
X	2004	2021
XIII	2007	2024
XIV	2008	2025

13-year broods

brood	one appearance	next appearance
XIX	2011	2024
XXII	2014	2027
XXIII	2015	2028

Glossary

attract: to draw toward oneself

burrow: to tunnel into the ground

decibel: a unit that measures loudness

emerge: to come out

exoskeleton: the hard covering on the outside of an animal's body that holds and guards the soft insides

larvae: bugs in an early stage of life that have a wormlike form

mate: to come together to make babies

mature: to grow into an adult

nutrient: something needed for growth and health

shed: to lose fur, hair, feathers, or skin

species: a group of animals that are all of the same kind

transparent: easily seen through

For More Information

Books

Hall, Margaret. *Cicadas.* Mankato, MN: Capstone Press, 2006.

Pringle, Laurence. *Cicadas! Strange and Wonderful.* Honesdale, PA: Boyds Mills Press, 2010.

Websites

Cicada
animals.nationalgeographic.com/animals/bugs/cicada/
Read more about the cicada.

Cicada Mania
www.cicadamania.com/cicadas/
Check out this website devoted to cicadas. It includes facts, brood updates, and tons of pictures.

How Cicadas Work
science.howstuffworks.com/environmental/life/zoology/insects-arachnids/cicada.htm
Want to learn even more about cicadas? Visit the How Stuff Works webpage about these loud insects.

Index